J
0.004
Luh

The Wampanoag Indians

by Bill Lund

Content Consultant:
Russel Peters, President
Mashpee Tribal Council

Bridgestone Books

an imprint of Capstone Press

Bridgestone Books are published by Capstone Press
818 North Willow Street, Mankato, Minnesota 56001
http://www.capstone-press.com

Library of Congress Cataloging-in-Publication Data
Lund, Bill, 1954-
    The Wampanoag Indians/by Bill Lund.
    p. cm.--(Native peoples)
    Includes bibliographical references and index.
    Summary: Provides an overview of the past and present lives of the Wampanoag Indians,
covering their daily life, customs, relations with the government and others, and more.
    ISBN 1-56065-564-X
    1. Wampanoag Indians--History--Juvenile literature. 2. Wampanoag Indians--Social life
and customs--Juvenile literature. [1. Wampanoag Indians. 2. Indians of North America--
Massachusetts.] I. Title. II. Series: Lund, Bill, 1954-   Native peoples.

E99.W2L86 1998
974.4'004973--dc21
                                                    97-6397
                                                      CIP
                                                      AC

Photo credits
Archive Photos, 18
Ben Klaffke, 10
John Madama, cover, 6, 12, 14, 16, 20
Plimoth Plantation/Ted Curtin, 8

Table of Contents

Map

Canada

U.S.A.

Where the Wampanoag used to live

Fast Facts

Today, many Wampanoag live like most other North Americans. In the past, they practiced a different way of life. Their food, homes, and clothing helped make them special. These facts tell how the Wampanoag used to live.

Food: The Wampanoag ate fish and animals. They also ate corn, beans, and squash.

Home: A Wampanoag home was called a wetu. A wetu was a round building with a round roof. The home was covered with tree bark and grasses.

Clothing: Most Wampanoag clothing was made from animal skins. Both men and women wore breechcloths. A breechcloth is a piece of animal skin. It passes between the legs and is tied with a belt. In the winter, the Wampanoag added more animal skins.

Language: The Wampanoag language is part of the Algonquian language family.

Past Location: The Wampanoag lived in the area that is now the northeastern United States. They lived in the area of southeastern Massachusetts.

Current Location: Today, many Wampanoags live in Rhode Island and Massachusetts.

Special Events: The Wampanoag gather together for Cranberry Day. They give thanks for all the cranberries they gather. They also hold clambakes. There they eat food to honor a special person.

The Wampanoag People

Long ago, Wampanoags lived in what is now southeastern Massachusetts. Today, many live in the same area. Others live in Rhode Island. They live on land that is set aside for them.

Today, the Wampanoag have a population of about 3,000. The U.S. government only recognizes the Gay Head tribe. A tribe is a group of people. They have the same family history, customs, and laws. Other Wampanoag tribes, such as the Mashpee, are applying for official recognition. Official recognition means the U.S. government allows the tribe to govern itself.

The Wampanoag hold special events throughout the year. Cranberry Day takes place on the second Tuesday of each October. The Wampanoag give thanks for the cranberries they will gather. Then they gather the cranberries and bring them back to town. Many people come to enjoy food, dancing, and drumming.

This boy is from the Mashpee tribe. The Mashpee tribe is applying for offical recognition.

Homes, Food, and Clothing

In the past, a Wampanoag home was called a wetu. A wetu was a round building with a round roof. Wampanoag men built a wetu by tying poles together. Then they covered the poles with grasses and tree bark. The Wampanoag also made longhouses. These buildings were used for tribal meetings.

Wampanoags ate food from the land and the sea. They hunted animals for food. They grew corn, beans, and squash. They saved these foods and ate them during winter. Wampanoags also caught shellfish, cod, bass, and lobsters.

Wampanoags made clothes from animal skins. Both men and women wore breechcloths. A breechcloth is a piece of animal skin. It passes between the legs and is tied with a belt. During winter, the Wampanoag added more animal skins. This helped keep them warm.

Long ago, the Wampanoag grew their own food, such as corn.

Wampanoag Crafts

The Wampanoag make many beautiful crafts. They make colorful pottery, jewelry, and paintings. Jewelry means objects that are worn for decoration.

Wampanoag pottery is made from clay. They find colored clays in cliffs near Gay Head, Massachusetts. Wampanoags shape the clay into pottery. They use the pottery for decoration.

The Mashpee Wampanoag make jewelry from Quahog shells. The shells are a deep purple color.

Some Wampanoag artists make paintings. Many show traditional Indian scenes. Some are paintings of nature.

The Wampanoag sell their crafts at powwows. A powwow is a gathering of Native Americans. Wampanoags hold their powwows during the summer and the fall.

Wampanoags make pottery from colored clay.

The Wampanoag Family

Families are important to the Wampanoag. The people form clans. A clan is a group of small related families. Each clan is guided by clan mothers. Other clan members choose the clan mothers. Each clan mother has a special skill. Some clan mothers work with children. Others make political decisions.

In the past, Wampanoag women kept their wetus clean. They also gathered and prepared food. They raised the children. The women taught the young girls these skills.

Wampanoag men taught young boys how to hunt and fish. They also taught them how to protect the tribe.

Long ago, the clans often moved when the seasons changed. In the summer, they stayed along the coast. In the winter, they moved into forests. Forests helped block out cold winds.

Families are important to the Wampanoag.

Wampanoag Religion

Followers of the Wampanoag religion believe in a Great Spirit. A religion is a set of beliefs people follow. The Wampanoag believe the Great Spirit is in all living things. They honor Mother Earth as the source of life. The Wampanoag believe all creatures are connected in the cycle of life. They respect each creature for its role in this cycle.

The unity circle is important to many Wampanoag. Unity means joining together. Friends and family members gather together for the unity circle. They spend several days eating special foods. They sing and dance around a fire. Firekeepers make sure the fire stays lit throughout the unity circle. The Supreme Medicine Man leads ceremonies at the unity circle.

Today, many Wampanoag still believe in their traditional religion. Other Wampanoag are members of Christian religions. Christianity is a religion based on the teachings of Christ.

The Supreme Medicine Man leads many ceremonies.

Wampanoag Government

There are two important leaders of the Wampanoag Nation. They are the Grand Sachem and the Supreme Medicine Man. The Grand Sachem is a governmental leader. The Supreme Medicine Man is a religious leader. Both provide wisdom and guidance to members of the tribe.

Today, the Wampanoag have a tribal council. Council members work with problems that affect the tribe. They work with schools and businesses. They answer questions about the law. They try to make things better for Wampanoag people.

Sometimes, the Wampanoag hold powwows. At the powwows, they talk about government issues. They also perform religious ceremonies. Some tribal members dance and sing while others beat drums. The drum is very important to the Wampanoag Nation. They say it is the heartbeat of the tribe.

Today, the Wampanoag have a tribal council.

King Philip's War

The Wampanoag were the first native people to meet the Pilgrims. The Pilgrims were English people who settled on Wampanoag land in 1620. The Pilgrims' crops would not grow. The Wampanoag taught them about the new land. The Wampanoag and English settlers celebrated the first Thanksgiving together.

Ossamiquin was a Wampanoag Massasoit. A Massasoit is a chief. He made a peace treaty with the new settlers. A treaty is an agreement between two nations. He also gave the English settlers land. The English did not honor their part of the treaty. Massasoit kept his part of the treaty.

Later, Metacomet became Massasoit. The English knew him as King Philip. Metacomet had seen the English take over Wampanoag land. He started a war with the English. King Philip's War lasted from 1675 to 1676. Metacomet was killed. The English won the war.

Metacomet was a Wampanoag Massasoit.

The Giant Maushop

The Wampanoag tell many stories called legends. Legends explain things in nature. The Giant Maushop was part of many Wampanoag legends.

Maushop was a giant who lived long ago. He lived high up on the cliffs. He was so tall that trees looked like weeds to him. He could eat a whole whale in a single meal.

One day, Maushop emptied the sand from his giant moccasins. The sand from each mocassin became an island. These islands are now known as Nantucket and Martha's Vineyard.

Sometimes Maushop came down from the cliffs. He taught the Wampanoag lessons. For example, sometimes Maushop had more fish than he could use. He gave the extra fish to the Wampanoag people. Maushop taught the Wampanoag about generosity through these actions. Generosity means sharing with people.

The Wampanoag still tell stories called legends.

Hands On: Ring and Pin

Wampanoag children played ring and pin for target practice. You can play ring and pin, too.

What You Need
- a six-inch (15-centimeter) stick or a new pencil that has never been sharpened
- 24-inch (61 centimeter) string
- a cardboard circle eight inches (20 centimeters) in diameter
- hole punch or scissors

What You Do
1. Cut a one-inch (about two-centimeter) hole in the center of the circle. The cardboard circle is your target.
2. Make a small hole near the edge of the target. Put one end of the string through this hole. Tie the string to the edge of the target.
3. Tie the other end of the string to the end of the stick with a tight knot.
4. To play, hold the stick and toss the target into the air. Use the stick to spear the middle hole. Keep the stick away from your face and from other people.
5. Give yourself five points for spearing the target with the stick or pencil.
6. Keep playing until you miss the hole. Then the next player has a turn.
7. The first player to 100 points wins.
8. You can play the game alone, too.

Words to Know

breechcloth (BREECH-klawth)—a piece of deerskin that passes between the legs; it is tied around the waist with a belt

Grand Sachem (GRAND SAY-chem)—an important religious leader

Massasoit (MASS-ah-soit)—a Wampanoag chief

unity circle (YOO-nit-ee SUR-kuhl)—a special gathering of family and friends

wetu (WEE-too)—a round building with a round roof that is covered with grass, leaves, or animal skins

Read More

Doherty, Katherine A. and Craig A. *The Wampanoag*. New York: Franklin Watts, 1995.

Peters, Russell M. *Clambake, A Wampanoag Tradition*. Minneapolis: Lerner Publications, 1992.

Weinstein-Farson, Laurie. *The Wampanoag*. New York: Chelsea House Publishers, 1989.

Useful Addresses

Wampanoag of Gay Head
State Road, RFD Box 137
Gay Head, MA 02535

Mashpee Wampanoag Indian Museum
13 Great Neck Road N
Mashpee, MA 02649

Internet Sites

New Bedford Ethnic Groups-Wampanoag
http://www.newbedford.com/ntvamerican.html

Native American Cultural Resources on the Internet
http://hanksville.phast.umass.edu/misc/
    NAculture.html

Index